You've Got This

A POCKET GUIDE FOR MATERNAL MENTAL HEALTH

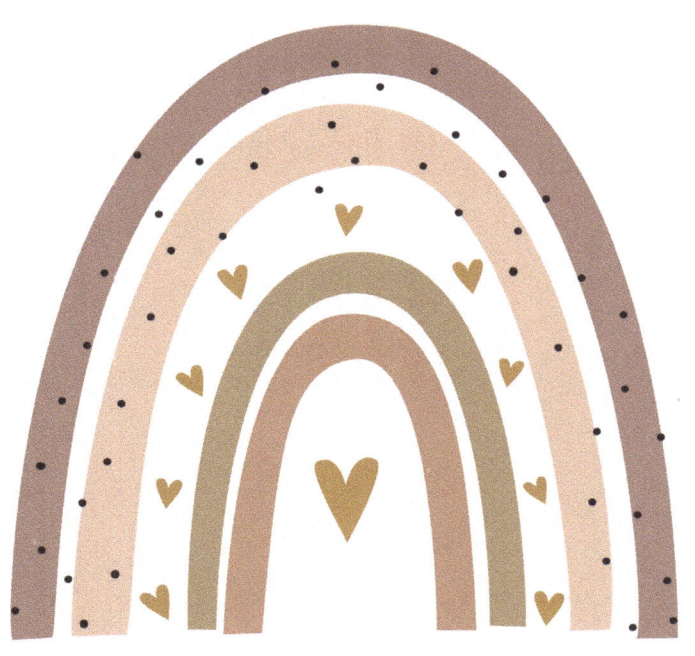

ROBIN GILES — & — JOY SUBRIN

You've Got This
© 2024 Robin Giles and Joy Subrin
All rights reserved.

ISBN: 978-1-953487-22-3

Printed in USA
Three Knolls Publishing | www.3knollspub.com

Praise for Y.G.T.

"Everyone should have a copy of this book."
- Sara N. Frye, OD, MPH & MOM!

"As a therapist supporting those experiencing perinatal mood disorders, this pocket guide gently provides essential information during a rapidly changing time. All new parents will benefit from this beautifully supportive tool!"
- Dr. Alison Sutton-Ryan,
Doctor of Behavioral Health

"This book is easy to read with helpful, concise suggestions for expectant moms to support their mental health and wellness!"
- Mara Gibney, RN
Public Health Antenatal Community Care

Praise for Y.G.T.

For all the women striving to do it all, this book offers a gentle reminder to slow down, care for themselves, and embrace this special time. A must read for every woman entering motherhood and for the loved ones supporting her on this journey."
-Andrea Moses, MD & MOM of Three

"This is a beautiful book offering valuable information and encouragement for women after they give birth. It offers practical strategies for coping and healing. This guide is a beacon of hope for those navigating the waters of postpartum depression. It's a great tool for any new mom!"
- Katy Hoeft, PA-C

Forward

Maternal mental health matters. During your pregnancy so much attention is given to physical changes, we encourage you to pay equal attention to your mental health. We hope that you will use this book as a guide to establish a mental health care plan.

You might be feeling anxious, lonely, afraid, excited or a mixture of many different emotions. Your journey is unique. Talk to your friends, family, and providers about your thoughts, feelings, and mental health during this period of transition.

These pearls of wisdom are our gift to you. They are a compilation of years of training and our experiences working with pregnant people and families just like yours. You've got this!

A special thank you to our own families who supported and believed in us along the way.

A

Ask for Help

Be specific in your asks.

Can you hold the baby for me? Can you pick up the groceries? Can we talk about our schedule for next week? Can you take the second nighttime feeding? Will you attend my next appointment with me?

What are your asks?
Take a moment to jot down your thoughts here:

_____

_____

_____

_____

B

Baby Blues

Baby blues typically occur very early after childbirth,
peaking around day four or five. It is a very common
and temporary set of symptoms that typically
resolve on their own in under two weeks.

Symptoms may include:
feelings of sadness, increased tiredness,
difficulty making decisions, and changes in
eating or sleeping habits. If your symptoms continue
more than two weeks, please contact your provider.
Reach out and talk to a trusted family member, friend,
or network for maternal mental health support.

You are not alone.

C
Compassion

Practicing self-compassion is key to nurturing yourself during times of change.

Have you acknowledged your strengths or accomplishments? Even the small steps count!

"I took a shower today!"
"I brushed my teeth today!"
"I attended a prenatal yoga class."
"I got a nap while the baby slept!"

What did you accomplish today or this week?

_____

_____

_____

D

Delivery
&
Care Services

You can save time and energy by using services and downloading digital apps that bring goods and services to you!

This is a time to invest and preserve your energy.

Examples: Laundry services, grocery delivery services, dog walking services, cleaning services, food delivery and even caregiving or doula services.

For the more budget conscious (which is many of us!), enlist a good friend to start a meal train or help you fill the freezer. One step further, visit webpages for major stores or products that you use and search for coupons, discount codes or programs for assistance; especially for moms of multiples!

E

Exercise

Get a natural mood boost by moving your body.
Go for a walk and explore nature.

The activation of your senses is a quick and easy
self-care activity -
can you hear the birds, see the clouds?

Just gentle movement can start you on this track.
Roll your shoulders, rotate your wrists.
You can individualize your pace or difficulty.

Your exercise routine will be different
during or after pregnancy.

Please be patient as your
sleep, energy and strength
are different right now.

F

Fourth Trimester!

Your recovery does not end the minute
you give birth! The fourth trimester is now
recognized as the crucial 12 weeks
following delivery that is filled with
adjustment, both physically and mentally.

You are officially in the time you were waiting for!

Please be kind to yourself as you adjust,
learn, grow, and explore this new world.

G
Gentle

Be gentle with yourself.
Nurture yourself with kind words
and encouraging thoughts.

Practice reading a positive affirmation or
write your own mantra for self-compassion.

"Rest is necessary."
"I am a work in progress."
"Just breath."
"Every day we grow, and I am learning."
"I am enough."

Add your positive affirmation:

_____

_____

_____

H

Healing

Healing takes time.

If something unexpected or traumatic occurred during
pregnancy or delivery,
you are not alone. Healing your mind
and body takes time.

This is hard work!!!!

Things may not be going as you envisioned,
take as much time as you need to adjust
physically and mentally.
Your timeline and recovery plan will be
different than your friends or neighbors.

See the resource page at the end
of this guide if you are looking for
additional support to heal from
a traumatic birth.

I

Insecure

Feeling insecure or unsure about yourself
is common. Feeling lonely or isolated?
You are not alone and you are learning as you go.

You can reach out and ask a friend
for support or join a maternal mental health
support group. It takes time and maybe
even a village to settle into your new role.

Find a supportive tribe for kinship!

J

Just Let It Be

Focus on yourself in the moment.
Practice mindfulness in times of increased stress.

For example: The laundry can wait,
replying to an e-mail or
social media posting can be paused.

You may need to let the nonessentials go,
for today. If you have met your limit,
just let it be for the moment.

K

Knowledge

We love this quote by Maya Angelou,
"Do your best until you know better; then do better."

Knowledge and education build confidence.
Check in with your local hospital for a class,
reading recommendations or a program
that fits for your next steps.

The library or your local clinic can be a
source for free pregnancy
or parenting literature.

Do not get overwhelmed with
the abundance of social media advice.
Choose one or two trusted resources.

L

Lovely

Lovely smells and luminous lighting.
Elevate your mood by creating a calming
or energizing space.

Grab a cup of chamomile tea,
pull a lavender flower from a garden,
set up an essential oil diffuser, dim the lights
or open the curtains.

You can create a space that
influences your mood.

M

Music

Sound is a powerful
way to heal, relax
or
rejuvenate.

Create your playlists
for pregnancy,
delivery
and
postpartum.

N

Nutrition

Food for mood is a critical part of health,
wellness, recovery, and life!

Think about the quick snacks you can
grab to feed and nurture your body and soul.

If friends of family are wondering
how to help you, ask for nutritional
snacks or meals.
Meal prep with a friend or your partner.

For example: Boil a few eggs,
bag-up a handful of nuts
or baby carrots, create wholesome
soups or stews in your crockpot.

O
Open Communication

Express your thoughts and feelings openly
and directly. Try a statement that starts
with the word "I."

For example:
I think, I feel, or I want.

Having a hard time talking,
maybe write it down and share it.

It is OK to not be OK.

Please communicate when you are struggling.

Who can you communicate with
on your care team?

For ideas, please see our resource pages!

P

Postpartum Depression and Anxiety

For many pregnant people this may be
their first experience with mood change
and it can be scary. Perinatal depression
is the most common complication of childbearing.

It is estimated that 1 in 7 women will
experience perinatal depression.
You can reduce the risk by knowing the signs
to watch for and establishing a care plan.

Prevention and intervention are key.
Talk to your provider about treatment options.

The recommendations may include individual
counseling, group therapy, medication,
or a combination of these things.

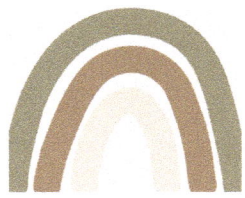

The common symptoms are: Two-weeks or more
of feeling irritable, lack of interest in baby,
hobbies, or things you previously enjoyed,
feeling hopeless, shame or guilt,
change in appetite, change in sleep, frequent worries
and possible worrisome thoughts of harming
yourself or baby.

Calling or texting a crisis line is an essential
component of a safety plan to include for any
antepartum or postpartum family.
Please see our resource pages at the end of this book.

What is your local crisis line?

_____

Q
Quiet Time

Have you become sensory overloaded?
Can you unplug from the digital
world for a block of time?

Even if you can't sleep, quiet your
mind for five-minutes of quintessential
quality quiet time.

For example: Listen to sounds of nature,
self-hand massage or request gentle touch
from a member of your support system.

R

Reality vs. Expectations

The reality is not what you see on the
magazine covers or social media!
The reality is you are adjusting to a new role,
changing sleep patterns and body changes.

This is a time of transformation,
and we don't have a glam squad!

You are beautiful just the way you are!
If you are struggling remember
it is likely temporary.

Stigma

In our society there is a stigma around maternal mental health and people are afraid to be labeled with a mental health diagnosis.

Gently allow yourself to let go if you are feeling ashamed or embarrassed.

Start a conversation with your provider, friends and family about your mood. Be your own advocate and identify your unique mental health needs.

Maternal mental health matters.

T

Transition

Now begins a journey of many changes.
Gains, losses, adjustments, grief,
joy, and new roles.
Acknowledge that you are
shifting and evolving.

Each day is a new day.

U
Unlimited

Your energy is not unlimited.

Envision a water pitcher or glass.
You have to take time to refill your glass
or pitcher! Be mindful when your glass is empty,
full or overflowing!

Use this pocket guide to cultivate ways
to refill your pitcher.

Visualization

Visualization is a mindfulness tool
that can reduce stress and increase relaxation.
Imagine a place in your mind
that offers you comfort and relaxation.

Imagine yourself at the beach, as the waves roll in...
breathe in what you crave. Breathe in feelings of calm,
peace and confidence.

Perhaps you imagine a field of flowers. As you
walk through the flowers, pick what you need.
Pick a flower for strength, one for gratitude and
another for appreciation. Keep picking flowers
until your bouquet is full of what you need.

You can also look up guided visualization
activities on popular phone apps or online.

Water

It seems simple to drink water, but it is
hard to drink enough water per day!
Hydration plays a role in physical health,
mental health, and brain functions.
An adequate water intake is essential for health

Try unsweetened herbal tea or sparkling water.
You can add fruit to your water to add flavor
and aromatics.

Staying hydrated is essential.

X

eXpert

Seek out an expert in maternal mental
health for individualized support,
guidance, and treatments to help
you through this milestone in your life.

Please say something. Help is available.

See our resource pages for ideas.

You've Got This

Believe in yourself! We believe in you!

You picked up this book to seek out
support and information, let this be a
springboard to your self-care plan.
This time of your life may be joyous
and at the same time challenging.

Save space for both things to be true.
You can be experiencing joy and challenges
at the same time.

Z

Catch Some ZZZzzzz's

Sleep is another essential layer of
self-care and health. Sleep is needed
for survival.

Getting better sleep can make a big difference
in regulating your mood.

Common ways to catch more ZZZ's include:

Dim the lights, cool your bedroom temperature,
monitor your time on electronic devices,
track your caffeine, try a gentle stretch
and listen to peaceful sounds.

Resources

American College of Obstetricians and Gynecologists
http://www.acog.org
The American College of Obstetricians and Gynecologists (ACOG) is a
professional organization for obstetricians - gynecologists. They produce
evidenced based practice guidelines for health care professionals. They
offer patient education materials and an online resource library.

Bluedot Project
https://www.thebluedotproject.org
The mission of TheBlueDotProject is to raise awareness of perinatal
mental health disorders. The blue dot is the symbol of perinatal mental
health survivorship, support and solidarity.

International Cesarean Awareness Network "ICAN"
http://www.ican-online.org
ICAN is a non-profit organization whose mission is to improve ma-
ternal-child health by reducing preventable cesareans via education,
support for those in cesarean recovery, and advocating for vaginal birth
after cesarean (VBAC).

International Marcé Society for Perinatal Mental Health
http://www.marcesociety.com
Marcé is an international, interdisciplinary organization dedicated to
supporting research and assistance around peripartum mental health for
mothers, fathers and their babies.

National Suicide and Crisis Hotline
If in crisis, please call your state or local hotline or
Text 988 if in The United States
https://988lifeline.org/

Resources

Maternal Mental Health Leadership Alliance
https://www.mmhla.org
They advocate for improved mental health during pregnancy
and in the postpartum period. They promote information to advance the
field of maternal mental health.

National Maternal Health Hotline
1- 833- TLC-MAMA
(1-833-TLC-6262) or website
http://www.mchb.hrsa.gov
The National Maternal Health Hotline provides 24/7 voice and text
support in English and Spanish and translation services in sixty
languages. Calls are answered by certified mental health
providers and peer specialists.

Postpartum Support International
1-800-944-4773 or Text "help" to 800- 944-4773,
For Spanish Text en Español: 971-203-7773
or website at @ http://www.postpartum.net
The purpose of this organization is to increase awareness among
public and professional communities about the emotional changes
women experience during pregnancy and postpartum. PSI offers 50 free
and virtual support groups. PSI offers training and education for providers.

Disclaimer

The information contained in this pocket guide is intended for
general consumer understanding and education only.
The pocket guide is not intended to be
a substitute for professional medical advice.

You should always seek the advice of your physician or
other qualified health provider with any questions or concerns
you may have regarding your health.

You are not alone and support is available.

Like this book?
We'd love to hear your comments.
Contact the authors @ YGTauthors@gmail.com

or

Publisher: www.3knollspub.com/JoyandRobin

www.ingramcontent.com/pod-product-compliance
Lightning Source LLC
Chambersburg PA
CBHW051651120626
46551CB00015B/2310